The Complete Poetical Works of Stephen Crane

Written by
Stephen Crane

2015

Table of Contents

THE BLACK RIDERS AND OTHER LINES - 6 -

- I - 7 -
- II - 8 -
- III - 9 -
- IV - 10 -
- V - 11 -
- VI - 12 -
- VII - 13 -
- VIII - 14 -
- IX - 15 -
- X - 16 -
- XI - 17 -
- XII - 18 -
- XIII - 19 -
- XIV - 20 -
- XV - 21 -
- XVI - 22 -
- XVII - 23 -
- XVIII - 24 -
- XIX - 25 -
- XX - 26 -
- XXI - 27 -
- XXII - 28 -
- XXIII - 29 -
- XXIV - 30 -
- XXV - 31 -
- XXVI - 32 -
- XXVII - 33 -
- XXVIII - 34 -

XXIX - 35 -
XXX - 36 -
XXXI - 37 -
XXXII - 38 -
XXXIII - 39 -
XXXIV - 40 -
XXXV - 41 -
XXXVI - 42 -
XXXVII - 43 -
XXXVIII - 44 -
XXXIX - 45 -
XL - 46 -
XLI - 47 -
XLII - 48 -
XLIII - 49 -
XLIV - 50 -
XLV - 51 -
XLVI - 52 -
XLVII - 53 -
XLVIII - 54 -
XLIX - 55 -
L - 57 -
LI - 58 -
LII - 59 -
LIII - 60 -
LIV - 61 -
LV - 62 -
LVI - 63 -
LVII - 64 -
LVIII - 65 -

LIX - 66 -
LX - 67 -
LXI - 68 -
LXII - 69 -
LXIII - 70 -
LXIV - 71 -
LXV - 72 -
LXVI - 73 -
LXVII - 74 -
LXVIII - 75 -
WAR IS KIND - 76 -

THE BLACK RIDERS AND OTHER LINES

I

Black Riders came from the sea.
There was clang and clang of spear and shield,
And clash and clash of hoof and heel,
Wild shouts and the wave of hair
In the rush upon the wind:
Thus the ride of Sin.

II

Three little birds in a row
Sat musing.
A man passed near that place.
Then did the little birds nudge each other.
They said, "He thinks he can sing."
They threw back their heads to laugh,
With quaint countenances
They regarded him.
They were very curious,
Those three little birds in a row.

III

In the desert
I saw a creature, naked, bestial,
Who, squatting upon the ground,
Held his heart in his hands,
And ate of it.
I said, "Is it good, friend?"
"It is bitter — bitter," he answered;
"But I like it
Because it is bitter,
And because it is my heart."

IV

Yes, I have a thousand tongues,
And nine and ninety-nine lie.
Though I strive to use the one,
It will make no melody at my will,
But is dead in my mouth.

V

Once there came a man
Who said,
"Range me all men of the world in rows."
And instantly
There was terrific clamor among the people
Against being ranged in rows.
There was a loud quarrel, world-wide.
It endured for ages;
And blood was shed
By those who would not stand in rows,
And by those who pined to stand in rows,
Eventually, the man went to death, weeping.
And those who staid in bloody scuffle
Knew not the great simplicity.

VI

God fashioned the ship of the world carefully
With the infinite skill of an All-Master
Made He the hull and the sails,
Held He the rudder
Ready for adjustment.
Erect stood He, scanning his work proudly.
Then — at fateful time — a Wrong called,
And God turned, heeding.
Lo, the ship, at this opportunity, slipped slyly,
Making cunning noiseless travel down the ways.
So that, forever rudderless, it went upon the seas
Going ridiculous voyages,
Making quaint progress,
Turning as with serious purpose
Before stupid winds.
And there were many in the sky
Who laughed at this thing.

VII

Mystic Shadow, bending near me,
Who art thou?
Whence come ye?
And — tell me — is it fair
Or is the truth bitter as eaten fire?
Tell me!
Fear not that I should quaver,
For I dare — I dare.
Then, tell me!

VIII

I looked here;
I looked there;
Nowhere could I see my love.
And — this time —
She was in my heart.
Truly, then, I have no complaint,
For though she be fair and fairer,
She is none so fair as she
In my heart.

IX

I stood upon a high place,
And saw, below, many devils
Running, leaping,
And carousing in sin.
One looked up, grinning,
And said, "Comrade! Brother!"

X

Should the wide world roll away,
Leaving black terror,
Limitless night,
Nor God, nor man, nor place to stand
Would be to me essential,
If thou and thy white arms were there,
And the fall to doom a long way.

XI

In a lonely place,
I encountered a sage
Who sat, all still,
Regarding a newspaper.
He accosted me:
"Sir, what is this?"
Then I saw that I was greater,
Aye, greater than this sage.
I answered him at once,
"Old, old man, it is the wisdom of the age."
The sage looked upon me with admiration.

XII

"and the sins of the fathers shall be
visited upon the heads of the children,
even unto the third and fourth
generation of them that hate me."
Well, then, I hate thee, Unrighteous Picture;
Wicked Image, I hate thee;
So, strike with thy vengeance
The heads of those little men
Who come blindly.
It will be a brave thing.

XIII

If there is a witness to my little life,
To my tiny throes and struggles,
He sees a fool;
And it is not fine for gods to menace fools.

XIV

There was crimson clash of war.
Lands turned black and bare;
Women wept;
Babes ran, wondering.
There came one who understood not these things.
He said, "Why is this?"
Whereupon a million strove to answer him.
There was such intricate clamor of tongues,
That still the reason was not.

XV

"Tell brave deeds of war."
Then they recounted tales, —
"There were stern stands
"And bitter runs for glory."
Ah, I think there were braver deeds.

XVI

Chanty, thou art a lie,
A toy of women,
A pleasure of certain men.
In the presence of justice,
Lo, the walls of the temple
Are visible
Through thy form of sudden shadows.

XVII

There were many who went in huddled procession,
They knew not whither;
But, at any rate, success or calamity
Would attend all in equality.
There was one who sought a new road.
He went into direful thickets,
And ultimately he died thus, alone;
But they said he had courage.

XVIII

In Heaven,
Some little blades of grass
Stood before God.
"What did you do?"
Then all save one of the little blades
Began eagerly to relate
The merits of their lives.
This one stayed a small way behind,
Ashamed.
Presently, God said,
"And what did you do?"
The little blade answered, "Oh, my Lord,
"Memory is bitter to me,
"For, if I did good deeds,
"I know not of them."
Then God, in all His splendor,
Arose from His throne.
"Oh, best little blade of grass!" He said.

XIX

A god in wrath
Was beating a man;
He cuffed him loudly
With thunderous blows
That rang and rolled over the earth.
All people came running.
The man screamed and struggled,
And bit madly at the feet of the god.
The people cried,
"Ah, what a wicked man!"
And —
"Ah, what a redoubtable god!"

XX

A learned man came to me once.
He said, "I know the way, — come."
And I was overjoyed at this.
Together we hastened.
Soon, too soon, were we
Where my eyes were useless,
And I knew not the ways of my feet
I clung to the hand of my friend;
But at last he cried, "I am lost."

XXI

There was, before me,
Mile upon mile
Of snow, ice, burning sand.
And yet I could look beyond all this,
To a place of infinite beauty;
And I could see the loveliness of her
Who walked in the shade of the trees.
When I gazed,
All was lost
But this place of beauty and her.
When I gazed,
And in my gazing, desired,
Then came again
Mile upon mile,
Of snow, ice, burning sand.

XXII

Once I saw Mountains angry,
And ranged in battle-front.
Against them stood a little man;
Aye, he was no bigger than my finger.
I laughed, and spoke to one near me,
"Will he prevail?"
"Surely," replied this other;
"His grandfathers beat them many times."
Then did I see much virtue in grandfathers, —
At least, for the little man
Who stood against the Mountains.

XXIII

Places among the stars,
Soft gardens near the sun,
Keep your distant beauty;
Shed no beams upon my weak heart.
Since she is here
In a place of blackness,
Not your golden days
Nor your silver nights
Can call me to you.
Since she is here
In a place of blackness,
Here I stay and wait.

XXIV

I saw a man pursuing the horizon;
Round and round they sped.
I was disturbed at this;
I accosted the man.
"It is futile," I said,
"You can never" —
"You lie," he cried,
And ran on.

XXV

Behold, the grave of a wicked man,
And near it, a stern spirit.
There came a drooping maid with violets,
But the spirit grasped her arm.
"No flowers for him," he said.
The maid wept:
"Ah, I loved him."
But the spirit, grim and frowning:
"No flowers for him."
Now, this is it —
If the spirit was just,
Why did the maid weep?

XXVI

There was set before me a mighty hill,
And long days I climbed
Through regions of snow.
When I had before me the summit-view,
It seemed that my labor
Had been to see gardens
Lying at impossible distances.

XXVII

A youth in apparel that glittered
Went to walk in a grim forest.
There he met an assassin
Attired all in garb of old days;
He, scowling through the thickets,
And dagger poised quivering,
Rushed upon the youth.
"Sir," said this latter,
"I am enchanted, believe me,
"To die, thus,
"In this medieval fashion,
"According to the best legends;
"Ah, what joy!"
Then took he the wound, smiling,
And died, content.

XXVIII

"Truth," said a traveller,
"Is a rock, a mighty fortress;
"Often have I been to it,
"Even to its highest tower,
"From whence the world looks black."
"Truth," said a traveller,
"Is a breath, a wind,
"A shadow, a phantom;
"Long have I pursued it,
"But never have I touched
"The hem of its garment."
And I believed the second traveller;
For truth was to me
A breath, a wind,
A shadow, a phantom,
And never had I touched
The hem of its garment.

XXIX

Behold, from the land of the farther suns
I returned.
And I was in a reptile-swarming place,
Peopled, otherwise, with grimaces,
Shrouded above in black impenetrableness.
I shrank, loathing,
Sick with it.
And I said to him,
"What is this?"
He made answer slowly,
"Spirit, this is a world;
"This was your home."

XXX

Supposing that I should have the courage
To let a red sword of virtue
Plunge into my heart,
Letting to the weeds of the ground
My sinful blood,
What can you offer me?
A gardened castle?
A flowery kingdom?
What? A hope?
Then hence with your red sword of virtue.

XXXI

Many workmen
Built a huge ball of masonry
Upon a mountain-top.
Then they went to the valley below,
And turned to behold their work.
"It is grand," they said;
They loved the thing.
Of a sudden, it moved:
It came upon them swiftly;
It crushed them all to blood.
But some had opportunity to squeal.

XXXII

Two or three angels
Came near to the earth.
They saw a fat church.
Little black streams of people
Came and went in continually.
And the angels were puzzled
To know why the people went thus,
And why they stayed so long within.

XXXIII

There was one I met upon the road
Who looked at me with kind eyes.
He said, "Show me of your wares."
And this I did,
Holding forth one.
He said, "It is a sin."
Then held I forth another;
He said, "It is a sin."
Then held I forth another;
He said, "It is a sin."
And so to the end;
Always he said, "It is a sin."
And, finally, I cried out,
"But I have none other."
Then did he look at me
With kinder eyes.
"Poor soul!" he said.

XXXIV

I stood upon a highway,
And, behold, there came
Many strange pedlers.
To me each one made gestures.
Holding forth little images, saying,
"This is my pattern of God.
"Now this is the God I prefer."
But I said, "Hence!
"Leave me with mine own,
"And take you yours away;
"I can't buy of your patterns of God,
"The little Gods you may rightly prefer."

XXXV

A man saw a ball of gold in the sky;
He climbed for it,
And eventually he achieved it —
It was clay.
Now this is the strange part:
When the man went to the earth
And looked again,
Lo, there was the ball of gold.
Now this is the strange part:
It was a ball of gold.
Aye, by the Heavens, it was a ball of gold.

XXXVI

I met a seer.
He held in his hands
The book of wisdom.
"Sir," I addressed him,
"Let me read."
"Child—" he began.
"Sir," I said,
"Think not that I am a child,
"For already I know much
"Of that which you hold.
"Aye, much."
He smiled.
Then he opened the book
And held it before me. —
Strange that I should have grown so suddenly blind.

XXXVII

On the horizon the peaks assembled;
And as I looked,
The march of the mountains began.
As they marched, they sang,
"Aye! We come! We come!"

XXXVIII

The ocean said to me once,
"Look!
"Yonder on the shore
"Is a woman, weeping.
"I have watched her.
"Go you and tell her this, —
"Her lover I have laid
"In cool green hall.
"There is wealth of golden sand
"And pillars, coral-red;
"Two white fish stand guard at his bier.
"Tell her this
"And more, —
"That the king of the seas
"Weeps too, old, helpless man.
"The bustling fates
"Heap his hands with corpses
"Until he stands like a child,
"With surplus of toys."

XXXIX

The livid lightnings flashed in the clouds;
The leaden thunders crashed.
A worshipper raised his arm.
"Hearken! Hearken! The voice of God!"
"Not so," said a man.
"The voice of God whispers in the heart
"So softly
"That the soul pauses,
"Making no noise,
"And strives for these melodies,
"Distant, sighing, like faintest breath,
"And all the being is still to hear."

XL

And you love me?
I love you.
You are, then, cold coward.
Aye; but, beloved,
When I strive to come to you,
Man's opinions, a thousand thickets,
My interwoven existence,
My life,
Caught in the stubble of the world
Like a tender veil, —
This stays me.
No strange move can I make
Without noise of tearing.
I dare not.
If love loves,
There is no world
Nor word.
All is lost
Save thought of love
And place to dream.
You love me?
I love you.
You are, then, cold coward.
Aye; but beloved —

XLI

Love walked alone.
The rocks cut her tender feet,
And the brambles tore her fair limbs.
There came a companion to her,
But, alas, he was no help,
For his name was Heart's Pain.

XLII

I walked in a desert.
And I cried,
"Ah, God, take me from this place!"
A voice said, "It is no desert."
I cried, "Well, but —
"The sand, the heat, the vacant horizon."
A voice said, "It is no desert."

XLIII

There came whisperings in the winds
"Good bye! Good bye!"
Little voices called in the darkness:
"Good bye! Good bye!"
Then I stretched forth my arms.
"No — no—"
There came whisperings in the wind:
"Good bye! Good bye!"
Little voices called in the darkness:
"Good bye! Good bye!"

XLIV

I was in the darkness;
I could not see my words
Nor the wishes of my heart.
Then suddenly there was a great light —
"Let me into the darkness again."

XLV

Tradition, thou art for suckling children,
Thou art the enlivening milk for babes;
But no meat for men is in thee.
Then —
But, alas, we all are babes.

XLVI

Many red devils ran from my heart
And out upon the page,
They were so tiny
The pen could mash them.
And many struggled in the ink.
It was strange
To write in this red muck
Of things from my heart.

XLVII

"Think as I think," said a man,
"Or you are abominably wicked;
"You are a toad."
And after I had thought of it,
I said, "I will, then, be a toad."

XLVIII

Once there was a man, —
Oh, so wise!
In all drink
He detected the bitter,
And in all touch
He found the sting.
At last he cried thus:
"There is nothing, —
"No life,
"No joy,
"No pain, —
"There is nothing save opinion,
"And opinion be damned."

XLIX

I stood musing in a black world,
Not knowing where to direct my feet.
And I saw the quick stream of men
Pouring ceaselessly,
Filled with eager faces,
A torrent of desire.
I called to them,
"Where do you go? What do you see?"
A thousand voices called to me.
A thousand fingers pointed.
"Look! Look! There!"
I know not of it.
But, lo! in the far sky shone a radiance
Ineffable, divine, —
A vision painted upon a pall;
And sometimes it was,
And sometimes it was not.
I hesitated.
Then from the stream
Came roaring voices,
Impatient:
"Look! Look! There!"
So again I saw,
And leaped, unhesitant,
And struggled and fumed
With outspread clutching fingers.
The hard hills tore my flesh;
The ways bit my feet.
At last I looked again.
No radiance in the far sky,
Ineffable, divine;

No vision painted upon a pall;
And always my eyes ached for the light.
Then I cried in despair,
"I see nothing! Oh, where do I go?"
The torrent turned again its faces:
"Look! Look! There!"
And at the blindness of my spirit
They screamed,
"Fool! Fool! Fool!"

L

You say you are holy,
And that
Because I have not seen you sin.
Aye, but there are those
Who see you sin, my friend.

LI

A man went before a strange god, —
The god of many men, sadly wise.
And the deity thundered loudly,
Fat with rage, and puffing,
"Kneel, mortal, and cringe
"And grovel and do homage
"To my particularly sublime majesty."
The man fled.
Then the man went to another god, —
The god of his inner thoughts.
And this one looked at him
With soft eyes
Lit with infinite comprehension,
And said, "My poor child!"

LII

Why do you strive for greatness, fool?
Go pluck a bough and wear it.
It is as sufficing.
My lord, there are certain barbarians
Who tilt their noses
As if the stars were flowers,
And thy servant is lost among their shoe-buckles.
Fain would I have mine eyes even with their eyes.
Fool, go pluck a bough and wear it.

LIII

I
Blustering god,
Stamping across the sky
With loud swagger,
I fear you not.
No, though from your highest heaven
You plunge your spear at my heart,
I fear you not.
No, not if the blow
Is as the lightning blasting a tree,
I fear you not, puffing braggart.
II
If thou can see into my heart
That I fear thee not,
Thou wilt see why I fear thee not,
And why it is right.
So threaten not, thou, with thy bloody spears,
Else thy sublime ears shall hear curses.
III
Withal, there is one whom I fear;
I fear to see grief upon that face.
Perchance, Friend, he is not your god;
If so, spit upon him.
By it you will do no profanity.
But I —
Ah, sooner would I die
Than see tears in those eyes of my soul.

LIV

"It was wrong to do this," said the angel.
"You should live like a flower,
"Holding malice like a puppy,
"Waging war like a lambkin."
"Not so," quoth the man
Who had no fear of spirits;
"It is only wrong for angels
"Who can live like the flowers,
"Holding malice like the puppies,
"Waging war like the lambkins."

LV

A man toiled on a burning road,
Never resting.
Once he saw a fat, stupid ass
Grinning at him from a green place.
The man cried out in rage,
"Ah! Do not deride me, fool!
"I know you —
"All day stuffing your belly,
"Burying your heart
"In grass and tender sprouts:
"It will not suffice you."
But the ass only grinned at him from the green place.

LVI

A man feared that he might find an assassin;
Another that he might find a victim.
One was more wise than the other.

LVII

With eye and with gesture
You say you are holy.
I say you lie;
For I did see you
Draw away your coats
From the sin upon the hands
Of a little child.
Liar!

LVIII

The sage lectured brilliantly.
Before him, two images:
"Now this one is a devil,
"And this one is me."
He turned away.
Then a cunning pupil
Changed the positions.
Turned the sage again:
"Now this one is a devil,
"And this one is me."
The pupils sat, all grinning,
And rejoiced in the game.
But the sage was a sage.

LIX

Walking in the sky,
A man in strange black garb
Encountered a radiant form.
Then his steps were eager;
Bowed he devoutly.
"My Lord," said he.
But the spirit knew him not.

LX

Upon the road of my life,
Passed me many fair creatures,
Clothed all in white, and radiant.
To one, finally, I made speech:
"Who art thou?"
But she, like the others,
Kept cowled her face,
And answered in haste, anxiously,
"I am Good Deed, forsooth;
"You have often seen me."
"Not uncowled," I made reply.
And with rash and strong hand,
Though she resisted,
I drew away the veil
And gazed at the features of Vanity
She, shamefaced, went on;
And after I had mused a time,
I said of myself,
"Fool!"

LXI

I
There was a man and a woman
Who sinned.
Then did the man heap the punishment
All upon the head of her,
And went away gayly.
II
There was a man and a woman
Who sinned.
And the man stood with her.
As upon her head, so upon his,
Fell blow and blow,
And all people screaming, "Fool!"
He was a brave heart.
III
He was a brave heart.
Would you speak with him, friend?
Well, he is dead,
And there went your opportunity.
Let it be your grief
That he is dead
And your opportunity gone;
For, in that, you were a coward.

LXII

There was a man who lived a life of fire.
Even upon the fabric of time,
Where purple becomes orange
And orange purple,
This life glowed,
A dire red stain, indelible;
Yet when he was dead,
He saw that he had not lived.

LXIII

There was a great cathedral.
To solemn songs,
A white procession
Moved toward the altar.
The chief man there
Was erect, and bore himself proudly.
Yet some could see him cringe,
As in a place of danger,
Throwing frightened glances into the air,
A-start at threatening faces of the past.

LXIV

Friend, your white beard sweeps the ground,
Why do you stand, expectant?
Do you hope to see it
In one of your withered days?
With your old eyes
Do you hope to see
The triumphal march of Justice?
Do not wait, friend
Take your white beard
And your old eyes
To more tender lands.

LXV

Once, I knew a fine song,
— It is true, believe me, —
It was all of birds,
And I held them in a basket;
When I opened the wicket,
Heavens! They all flew away.
I cried, "Come back, little thoughts!"
But they only laughed.
They flew on
Until they were as sand
Thrown between me and the sky.

LXVI

If I should cast off this tattered coat,
And go free into the mighty sky;
If I should find nothing there
But a vast blue,
Echoless, ignorant, —
What then?

LXVII

God lay dead in Heaven;
Angels sang the hymn of the end;
Purple winds went moaning,
Their wings drip-dripping
With blood
That fell upon the earth.
It, groaning thing,
Turned black and sank.
Then from the far caverns
Of dead sins
Came monsters, livid with desire.
They fought,
Wrangled over the world,
A morsel.
But of all sadness this was sad, —
A woman's arms tried to shield
The head of a sleeping man
From the jaws of the final beast.

LXVIII

A spirit sped
Through spaces of night;
And as he sped, he called,
"God! God!"
He went through valleys
Of black death-slime,
Ever calling,
"God! God!"
Their echoes
From crevice and cavern
Mocked him:
"God! God! God!"
Fleetly into the plains of space
He went, ever calling,
"God! God!"
Eventually, then, he screamed,
Mad in denial,
"Ah, there is no God!"
A swift hand,
A sword from the sky,
Smote him,
And he was dead.

WAR IS KIND

Do not weep, maiden, for war is kind.
Because your lover threw wild hands toward the sky
And the affrighted steed ran on alone,
Do not weep.
War is kind.
Hoarse, booming drums of the
regiment,
Little souls who thirst for fight,
These men were born to drill and die.
The unexplained glory files above
them,
Great is the battle-god, great, and his
kingdom — ;
A field where a thousand corpses lie.
Do not weep, babe, for war is kind.
Because your father tumbled in the yellow
trenches,
Raged at his breast, gulped and died,
Do not weep.
War is kind.
Swift blazing flag of the regiment,
Eagle with crest of red and gold,
These men were born to drill and die.
Point for them the virtue of the slaughter,
Make plain to them the excellence of killing
And a field where a thousand corpses
lie.
Mother whose heart hung humble as a button
On the bright splendid shroud of your son,
Do not weep.
War is kind.
What says the sea, little shell?
"What says the sea?

"Long has our brother been silent to us,
"Kept his message for the ships,
"Awkward ships, stupid ships."
"The sea bids you mourn, O Pines,
"Sing low in the moonlight.
"He sends tale of the land of doom,
"Of place where endless falls
"A rain of women's tears,
"And men in grey robes —
"Men in grey robes —
"Chant the unknown pain."
"What says the sea, little shell?
"What says the sea?
"Long has our brother been silent to us,
"Kept is message for the ships,
"Puny ships, silly ships."
"The sea bids you teach, O Pines,
"Sing low in the moonlight;
"Teach the gold of patience,
"Cry gospel of gentle hands,
"Cry a brotherhood of hearts.
"The sea bids you teach, O Pines."
"And where is the reward, little shell?
"What says the sea?
"Long has our brother been silent to us,
"Kept his message for the ships,
"Puny ships, silly ships."
"No word says the sea, O Pines,
"No word says the sea.
"Long will your brother be silent to you,
"Keep his message for the ships,
"O puny ships, silly pines."
To the maiden
The sea was blue meadow,
Alive with little froth-people

Singing.
To the sailor, wrecked,
The sea was dead grey walls
Superlative in vacancy,
Upon which nevertheless at fateful time
Was written
The grim hatred of nature.
A little ink more or less!
It surely can't matter?
Even the sky and the opulent sea,
The plains and the hills, aloof,
Hear the uproar of all these books.
But it is only a little ink more or less.
What?
You define me God with these trinkets?
Can my misery meal on an ordered walking
Of surpliced numskulls?
And a fanfare of lights?
Or even upon the measured pulpitings
Of the familiar false and true?
Is this God?
Where, then is hell?
Show me some bastard mushrooms
Sprung from a pollution of blood.
It is better.
Where is God?
"Have you ever made a just man?"
"Oh, I have made three," answered
God,
"But two of them are dead,
"And the third —
"Listen! Listen!
"And you will hear the thud of his defeat."
I explain the silvered passing of a ship
at night,

The sweep of each sad lost wave,
The dwindling boom of the steel thing's striving,
The little cry of a man to a man,
A shadow falling across the greyer night,
And the sinking of the small star;
Then the waste, the far waste of waters,
And the soft lashing of black waves
For long and in loneliness.
Remember, thou, O ship of love,
Thou leavest a far waste of waters,
And the soft lashing of black waves
For long and in loneliness.
"I have heard the sunset song of the
birches,
"A white melody in the silence,
"I have seen a quarrel of the pines.
"At nightfall
"The little grasses have rushed by me
"With the wind men.
"These things have I lived," quoth the
maniac,
"Possessing only eyes and ears.
"But you —
"You don green spectacles before you look at roses."
Fast rode the knight
With spurs, hot and reeking,
Ever waving an eager sword,
"To save my lady!"
Fast rode the knight,
And leaped from saddle to war.
Men of steel flickered and gleamed
Like riot of silver lights,
And the gold of the knight's good banner
Still waved on a castle wall.
. . . .

A horse,
Blowing, staggering, bloody thing,
Forgotten at foot of castle wall.
A horse
Dead at foot of castle wall.
Forth went the candid man
And spoke freely to the wind —
When he looked about him he was in a far
strange country.
Forth went the candid man
And spoke freely to the stars —
Yellow light tore sight from his eye.
"My good fool," said a learned bystander,
"Your operations are mad."
"You are too candid," cried the candid man.
And when his stick left the head of the
learned bystander
It was two sticks.
You tell me this is God?
I tell you this is a printed list,
A burning candle and an ass.
On the desert
A silence from the moon's deepest
valley.
Fire rays fall athwart the robes
Of hooded men, squat and dumb.
Before them, a woman
Moves to the blowing of shrill whistles
And distant thunder of drums,
While mystic things, sinuous, dull with
terrible color,
Sleepily fondle her body
Or move at her will, swishing stealthily over
the sand.
The snakes whisper softly;

The whispering, whispering snakes,
Dreaming and swaying and staring,
But always whispering, softly whispering.
The wind streams from the lone reaches
Of Arabia, solemn with night,
And the wild fire makes shimmer of blood
Over the robes of the hooded men
Squat and dumb.
Bands of moving bronze, emerald, yellow,
Circle the throat and arms of her,
And over the sands serpents move warily
Slow, menacing and submissive,
Swinging to the whistles and drums,
The whispering, whispering snakes,
Dreaming and swaying and staring,
But always whispering, softly whispering.
The dignity of the accursed;
The glory of slavery, despair, death,
Is in the dance of the whispering snakes.
A newspaper is a collection of half-injustices
Which, bawled by boys from mile to mile,
Spreads its curious opinion
To a million merciful and sneering men,
While families cuddle the joys of the fireside
When spurred by tale of dire lone agony.
A newspaper is a court
Where every one is kindly and unfairly tried
By a squalor of honest men.
A newspaper is a market
Where wisdom sells its freedom
And melons are crowned by the crowd.
A newspaper is a game
Where his error scores the player victory
While another's skill wins death.
A newspaper is a symbol;

It is fetless life's chronical,
A collection of loud tales
Concentrating eternal stupidities,
That in remote ages lived unhaltered,
Roaming through a fenceless world.
The wayfarer,
Perceiving the pathway to truth,
Was struck with astonishment.
It was thickly grown with weeds.
"Ha," he said,
"I see that none has passed here
"In a long time."
Later he saw that each weed
Was a singular knife.
"Well," he mumbled at last,
"Doubtless there are other roads."
A slant of sun on dull brown walls,
A forgotten sky of bashful blue.
Toward God a mighty hymn,
A song of collisions and cries,
Rumbling wheels, hoof-beats, bells,
Welcomes, farewells, love-calls, final moans,
Voices of joy, idiocy, warning, despair,
The unknown appeals of brutes,
The chanting of flowers,
The screams of cut trees,
The senseless babble of hens and wise men —
A cluttered incoherency that says at the
stars;
"O God, save us!"
Once a man clambering to the housetops
Appealed to the heavens.
With a strong voice he called to the deaf
spheres;
A warrior's shout he raised to the suns.

Lo, at last, there was a dot on the clouds,
And — at last and at last —
— God — the sky was filled with armies.
There was a man with tongue of wood
Who essayed to sing,
And in truth it was lamentable.
But there was one who heard
The clip-clapper of this tongue of wood
And knew what the man
Wished to sing,
And with that the singer was content.
The successful man has thrust himself
Through the water of the years,
Reeking wet with mistakes, —
Bloody mistakes;
Slimed with victories over the lesser,
A figure thankful on the shore of money.
Then, with the bones of fools
He buys silken banners
Limned with his triumphant face;
With the skins of wise men
He buys the trivial bows of all.
Flesh painted with marrow
Contributes a coverlet,
A coverlet for his contented slumber.
In guiltless ignorance, in ignorant guilt,
He delivered his secrets to the riven multitude.
"Thus I defended: Thus I wrought."
Complacent, smiling,
He stands heavily on the dead.
Erect on a pillar of skulls
He declaims his trampling of babes;
Smirking, fat, dripping,
He makes speech in guiltless ignorance,
Innocence.

In the night
Grey heavy clouds muffled the valleys,
And the peaks looked toward God alone.
"O Master that movest the wind with a
finger,
"Humble, idle, futile peaks are we.
"Grant that we may run swiftly across
the world
"To huddle in worship at Thy feet."
In the morning
A noise of men at work came the clear blue miles,
And the little black cities were apparent.
"O Master that knowest the meaning of raindrops,
"Humble, idle, futile peaks are we.
"Give voice to us, we pray, O Lord,
"That we may sing Thy goodness to the sun."
In the evening
The far valleys were sprinkled with tiny lights.
"O Master,
"Thou that knowest the value of kings and birds,
"Thou hast made us humble, idle, futile peaks.
"Thous only needest eternal patience;
"We bow to Thy wisdom, O Lord —
"Humble, idle, futile peaks."
In the night
Grey heavy clouds muffles the valleys,
And the peaks looked toward God alone.
The chatter of a death-demon from a tree-top.
Blood — blood and torn grass —
Had marked the rise of his agony —
This lone hunter.
The grey-green woods impassive
Had watched the threshing of his limbs.
A canoe with flashing paddle,
A girl with soft searching eyes,

A call: "John!"
. . . .
Come, arise, hunter!
Can you not hear?
The chatter of a death-demon from a tree-top.
The impact of a dollar upon the heart
Smiles warm red light,
Sweeping from the hearth rosily upon the
white table,
With the hanging cool velvet shadows
Moving softly upon the door.
The impact of a million dollars
Is a crash of flunkys,
And yawning emblems of Persia
Cheeked against oak, France and a sabre,
The outcry of old beauty
Whored by pimping merchants
To submission before wine and chatter.
Silly rich peasants stamp the carpets of men,
Dead men who dreamed fragrance and light
Into their woof, their lives;
The rug of an honest bear
Under the feet of a cryptic slave
Who speaks always of baubles,
Forgetting state, multitude, work, and state,
Champing and mouthing of hats,
Making ratful squeak of hats,
Hats.
A man said to the universe:
"Sir, I exist!"
"However," replied the universe,
"The fact has not created in me
"A sense of obligation."
When the prophet, a complacent fat
man,

Arrived at the mountain-top,
He cried: "Woe to my knowledge!
"I intended to see good white lands
"And bad black lands,
"But the scene is grey."
There was a land where lived no
violets.
A traveller at once demanded: "Why?"
The people told him:
"Once the violets of this place spoke thus:
"'Until some woman freely give her lover
"'To another woman
"'We will fight in bloody scuffle.'"
Sadly the people added:
"There are no violets here."
There was one I met upon the road
Who looked at me with kind eyes.
He said: "Show me of your wares."
And I did,
Holding forth one,
He said: "It is a sin."
Then I held forth another.
He said: "It is a sin."
Then I held forth another.
He said: "It is a sin."
And so to the end.
Always He said: "It is a sin."
At last, I cried out:
"But I have non other."
He looked at me
With kinder eyes.
"Poor soul," he said.
Aye, workman, make me a dream,
A dream for my love.
Cunningly weave sunlight,

Breezes, and flowers.
Let it be of the cloth of meadows.
And — good workman —
And let there be a man walking thereon.
Each small gleam was a voice,
A lantern voice —
In little songs of carmine, violet, green, gold.
A chorus of colors came over the water;
The wondrous leaf-shadow no longer wavered,
No pines crooned on the hills,
The blue night was elsewhere a silence,
When the chorus of colors came over the water,
Little songs of carmine, violet, green, gold.
Small glowing pebbles
Thrown on the dark plane of evening
Sing good ballads of God
And eternity, with soul's rest.
Little priests, little holy fathers,
None can doubt the truth of hour hymning.
When the marvellous chorus comes over the water,
Songs of carmine, violet, green, gold.
The trees in the garden rained flowers.
Children ran there joyously.
They gathered the flowers
Each to himself.
Now there were some
Who gathered great heaps —
Having opportunity and skill —
Until, behold, only chance blossoms
Remained for the feeble.
Then a little spindling tutor
Ran importantly to the father, crying:
"Pray, come hither!

"See this unjust thing in your garden!"
But when the father had surveyed,
He admonished the tutor:
"Not so, small sage!
"This thing is just.
"For, look you,
"Are not they who possess the flowers
"Stronger, bolder, shrewder
"Than they who have none?
"Why should the strong —
"The beautiful strong —
"Why should they not have the flowers?
Upon reflection, the tutor bowed to the ground.
"My lord," he said,
"The stars are displaced
"By this towering wisdom."

INTRIGUE

Thou art my love,
And thou art the peace of sundown
When the blue shadows soothe,
And the grasses and the leaves sleep
To the song of the little brooks,
Woe is me.

Thou art my love,
And thou art a strorm
That breaks black in the sky,
And, sweeping headlong,
Drenches and cowers each tree,
And at the panting end
There is no sound
Save the melancholy cry of a single owl —
Woe is me!

Thou are my love,
And thou art a tinsel thing,

And I in my play
Broke thee easily,
And from the little fragments
Arose my long sorrow —
Woe is me.
Thou art my love,
And thou art a wary violet,
Drooping from sun-caresses,
Answering mine carelessly —
Woe is me.
Thou art my love,
And thou art the ashes of other men's love,
And I bury my face in these ashes,
And I love them —
Woe is me.
Thou art my love,
And thou art the beard
On another man's face —
Woe is me.
Thou art my love,
And thou art a temple,
And in this temple is an altar,
And on this altar is my heart —
Woe is me.
Thou art my love,
And thou art a wretch.
Let these sacred love-lies choke thee,
From I am come to where I know your lies
as truth
And you truth as lies —
Woe is me.
Thou art my love,
And thou art a priestess,
And in they hand is a bloody dagger,
And my doom comes to me surely —

Woe is me.
Thou art my love,
And thou art a skull with ruby eyes,
And I love thee —
Woe is me.
Thou art my love,
And I doubt thee.
And if peace came with thy murder
Then would I murder —
Woe is me.
Thou art my love,
And thou art death,
Aye, thou art death
Black and yet black,
But I love thee,
I love thee —
Woe, welcome woe, to me.
Love, forgive me if I wish you grief,
For in your grief
You huddle to my breast,
And for it
Would I pay the price of your grief.
You walk among men
And all men do not surrender,
And thus I understand
That love reaches his hand
In mercy to me.
He had your picture in his room,
A scurvy traitor picture,
And he smiled
— Merely a fat complacence of men who
know fine women —
And thus I divided with him
A part of my love.
Fool, not to know that thy little shoe

Can make men weep!
— Some men weep.
I weep and I gnash,
And I love the little shoe,
The little, little shoe.
God give me medals,
God give me loud honors,
That I may strut before you, sweetheart,
And be worthy of —
The love I bear you.
Now let me crunch you
With full weight of affrighted love.
I doubted you
— I doubted you —
And in this short doubting
My love grew like a genie
For my further undoing.
Beware of my friends,
Be not in speech too civil,
For in all courtesy
My weak heart sees spectres,
Mists of desire
Arising from the lips of my chosen;
Be not civil.
The flower I gave thee once
Was incident to a stride,
A detail of a gesture,
But search those pale petals
And see engraven thereon
A record of my intention.
Ah, God, the way your little finger moved,
As you thrust a bare arm backward
And made play with your hair
And a comb, a silly gilt comb
— Ah, God — that I should suffer

Because of the way a little finger moved.
Once I saw thee idly rocking
— Idly rocking —
And chattering girlishly to other girls,
Bell-voiced, happy,
Careless with the stout heart of unscarred womanhood,
And life to thee was all light melody.
I thought of the great storms of love as I knew it,
Torn, miserable, and ashamed of my open sorrow,
I thought of the thunders that lived in my head,
And I wish to be an ogre,
And hale and haul my beloved to a castle,
And make her mourn with my mourning.
Tell me why, behind thee,
I see always the shadow of another lover?
Is it real,
Or is this the thrice damned memory of a better happiness?
Plague on him if he be dead,
Plague on him if he be alive —
A swinish numskull
To intrude his shade
Always between me and my peace!
And yet I have seen thee happy with me.
I am no fool
To poll stupidly into iron.
I have heard your quick breaths
And seen your arms writhe toward me;
At those times
— God help us —
I was impelled to be a grand knight,

And swagger and snap my fingers,
And explain my mind finely.
Oh, lost sweetheart,
I would that I had not been a grand knight.
I said: "Sweetheart."
Thou said'st: "Sweetheart."
And we preserved an admirable mimicry
Without heeding the drip of the blood
From my heart.
I heard thee laugh,
And in this merriment
I defined the measure of my pain;
I knew that I was alone,
Alone with love,
Poor shivering love,
And he, little sprite,
Came to watch with me,
And at midnight,
We were like two creatures by a dead camp-
fire.
I wonder if sometimes in the dusk,
When the brave lights that gild thy
evenings
Have not yet been touched with flame,
I wonder if sometimes in the dusk
Thou rememberest a time,
A time when thou loved me
And our love was to thee thy all?
Is the memory rubbish now?
An old gown
Worn in an age of other fashions?
Woe is me, oh, lost one,
For that love is now to me
A supernal dream,
White, white, white with many suns.

Love met me at noonday,
— Reckless imp,
To leave his shaded nights
And brave the glare, —
And I saw him then plainly
For a bungler,
A stupid, simpering, eyeless bungler,
Breaking the hearts of brave people
As the snivelling idiot-boy cracks his bowl,
And I cursed him,
Cursed him to and fro, back and forth,
Into all the silly mazes of his mind,
But in the end
He laughed and pointed to my breast,
Where a heart still beat for thee, beloved.
I have seen thy face aflame
For love of me,
Thy fair arms go mad,
Thy lips tremble and mutter and rave.
And — surely —
This should leave a man content?
Thou lovest not me now,
But thou didst love me,
And in loving me once
Thou gavest me an eternal privilege,
For I can think of thee.

CPSIA information can be obtained
at www.ICGtesting.com
Printed in the USA
LVHW050606060721
691876LV00018B/3157